Qigong for Christians:

A Christ-Centered Healing Meditation

Qigong for Christians:

A Christ-Centered Healing Meditation

By Sylvia

XULON PRESS

Xulon Press
2301 Lucien Way #415
Maitland, FL 32751
407.339.4217
www.xulonpress.com

© 2019 by Sylvia

All rights reserved solely by the author. The author guarantees all contents are original and do not infringe upon the legal rights of any other person or work. No part of this book may be reproduced in any form without the permission of the author. The views expressed in this book are not necessarily those of the publisher.

Scripture quotations are taken from the Holy Bible, New Living Translation, (NLT) copyright © 1996, 2004, 2007, 2013 by Tyndale House Foundation. Used by permission of Tyndale House Publishers, Inc., Carol Stream, Illinois 60188. All rights reserved.

Qigong procedural and other references are made and used by permission of Master Chunyi Lin; *Born a Healer*; Spring Forest Publishing; October 2005, United States of America.

And online: www.springforestqigong.com.

Master Chunyi Lin. Healing Connections audio tele-seminar. www.springforestqigong.com. 2018.

Master Chunyi Lin. www.bornahealer.com.

Printed in the United States of America.

ISBN-13: 978-1-54567-234-1

Table of Contents

About the Author vii
Acknowledgements ix
General Overview 1
Background Information on Qigong 3
How to Use Qigong for Christians 5
Disclaimer 9
Terminology Used in
Qigong for Christians and Definitions 11
Procedure with Applicable Bible Verses 13
Bibliography 35

About the Author

Sylvia, aka Carole S. Mazzone, RN, MSN, APRN-bc, has worked in the medical field since 1994, serving her patients as a nurse practitioner for the past thirteen years of her medical career. By the second grade, she knew that her calling was to be a nurse, to help her patients get better so they could better live and enjoy their lives.

Since 2008, Sylvia has been honored and privileged to be a student of Master Chunyi Lin, the founder of Spring Forest Qigong. Qigong is a meditation practice with a history in China, where you are regarded as a whole person—Heart, Mind, Body, and Spirit. In the practice of Spring Forest Qigong, the purpose is to remove the energy blockages in the energy channels of the body and to balance, restore, and maintain the flow of energy throughout the body for improved health. Master Chunyi Lin teaches Spring Forest Qigong with a multi-cultural approach.

As a born-again Christian, Sylvia found herself making adjustments to the way she practiced Spring Forest Qigong meditation, in order to make it more user-friendly for her Christian worldview. As she read and studied her Bible, Sylvia created a Jesus-centered Qigong healing meditation. Before long, she came to understand that, just as God had called her to be a nurse, she also feels a calling to share with others this Jesus-centered form of healing meditation—*Qigong for Christians*.

Acknowledgements

I wish to thank Tyndale House Publishers, Inc. for the New Living Translation (NLT) of the Holy Bible. It is easy to understand yet well delivers the biblical meanings. I thank Tyndale House Publishers for permitting me to use Bible verse references from the Holy Bible, New Living Translation, in my writing of *Qigong for Christians*.

I wish to acknowledge and thank my Spring Forest Qigong mentor, Master Chunyi Lin, for making Spring Forest Qigong available. I thank him for his support of my purpose to create a user-friendly form of *Qigong for Christians*.

Above all, I wish to thank my Lord Jesus Christ for His inspiration, presence, and guidance in my life. I thank the Lord for the gifts of the Holy Spirit and for the love, healing, forgiveness, and salvation He gives to His children of the Light.

General Overview

This nonfiction Christian help guide is to enlighten readers to the healing meditation of Qigong, an ancient practice from China. Using familiar steps from Qigong, combined with scriptural references, the author demonstrates how readers can do *Qigong for Christians* meditation and feel God's divine healing in their bodies, minds, and spirits.

The author carefully explains every step of the meditation, defining terms and statements so readers unfamiliar with Qigong can easily follow along and learn. Through the author's attention to detail in explaining the steps, it is clear that she respects the Qigong meditation and believes, when done right, that it can bring relief and clarity to the person.

The scripture references, which accompany each step of the healing meditation, illuminate how the presence of God can be felt while practicing the meditation. Each step is centered on glorifying and praising God. The Bible references bring to light the blessings of God to His children, while also being resources to guide the readers to stay centered in the Bible while meditating.

Background Information on Qigong

In Chinese, the word Qigong means, literally, "Life Energy Cultivation." Qigong is a holistic system of body postures and movement, breathing, and meditation used for the purposes of health and spirituality, with roots in Chinese medicine and philosophy. It has traditionally been viewed as a practice to cultivate and balance Qi, which is translated as "Life Energy."

Qigong practice involves movements; deep, rhythmic breathing; and a calm, meditative state of mind. It is now practiced worldwide for relaxation, preventative medicine, self-healing, alternative medicine, meditation, spirituality, and self-cultivation.

Qigong's roots are in ancient Chinese culture, dating back about four thousand years or more. There are many forms of Qigong. It is used in traditional Chinese medicine for prevention and cures, in Confucianism for longevity and moral character, and in Daoism and Buddhism as a meditation practice for higher awareness and spiritual enlightenment.

Therapeutically, Qigong can be used as a self-care practice or as a treatment done by one person on another. It utilizes meditation, breath awareness, and visualization; and it focuses on balancing the flow of Qi in the meridians and other body channels.

In Buddhist traditions, the aim is to still the mind through focus on the Eternal, and spiritual enlightenment. In the Confucius tradition, the goal is awareness of morality.

In China, Qigong has been recognized as a "standard medical technique" since 1989. According to the Chinese medical Qigong textbook, some of the many physiological benefits of Qigong are: improved respiratory, cardiovascular, and neuro-physiological functions, including improved mood, decreased stress and anxiety, serenity, mental clarity, and happiness.

Today, some integrative medicine practitioners use Qigong in countries other than China, including the United States, to complement conventional medical treatment based on the effectiveness and safety of the practice. It is generally seen as safe across diverse populations, with no adverse effects observed in clinical trials (en.m.Wikipedia.org, online cited 3-29-19; Wikipedia, "The Free Encyclopedia", English; The Wikimedia Foundation, Inc. online cited 6-15-19.).

How to Use Qigong for Christians

I have presented *Qigong for Christians* as a twelve-step procedure. Along with similarities to other world religions, such as the virtues of love, kindness, and forgiveness, there are also many special features which distinguish Christianity from other world views. While these are numerous, I will point out a few important distinctive aspects of Christianity to keep in mind while doing *Qigong for Christians*:

1.) When we trust in Jesus, we are made right with God.

> Romans 3:22   We are made right in God's sight when we trust in Jesus Christ to take away our sins.
>
> Romans 3:25   …We are made right with God when we believe that Jesus shed his blood, sacrificing his life for us.
>
> Romans 10:4   For Christ has accomplished the whole purpose of the law. All who believe in Him are made right with God.
>
> Hebrews 6:53   And so, dear brothers and sisters, we can boldly enter heaven's Most Holy Place because of the blood of Jesus.

2.) Through faith and belief that Jesus Christ died on the cross for our sins and was raised from the dead; and by His blood shed for us, we may confess our sins and be graciously forgiven. Thus, we are saved for all eternity.

> Romans 4:24-25 …God will also declare us to be righteous if we believe in God, who brought Jesus our Lord back from the dead. He was handed over to die because of our sins, and He was raised from the dead to make us right with God.
>
> Romans 6:23 For the wages of sin is death, but the free gift of God is eternal life through Christ Jesus our Lord.
>
> 1 John 1:7 But if we are living in the Light of God's presence, just as Christ is, then we have fellowship with each other; and the blood of Jesus, His Son, cleanses us from every sin.

3.) When we belong to Jesus, we are delivered. This freedom comes to us by God's wonderful kindness and grace.

> Ephesians 1:7 So we praise God for the wonderful kindness he has poured out on us because we belong to his dearly loved Son. He is so rich in kindness that He purchased our freedom through the blood of His Son, and our sins are forgiven.
>
> Romans 6:14 Sin is no longer your master…instead, you are free by God's grace.

In doing *Qigong for Christians*, it is important that we call upon our only true God: the Father, the Son, and the Holy Spirit, through Jesus Christ, our Lord and Savior.

Along with each of the twelve steps of *Qigong for Christians*, you will also see relevant Bible verses. As you do the steps of *Qigong for Christians*, call upon our Lord, Master Healer, Jesus Christ, to help you do your healing meditation. Feel His presence with you as you pray to Him and as you read the applicable Bible verses.

Notice your perceptions during or immediately following your Jesus-centered Qigong meditation. Jesus hears your prayers; you may possibly observe something. Examples of something one can perceive are, but are not limited to:

A lit-up cross,

A past occurrence that will be helpful to you by becoming aware of it,

A helpful inspiration from the Holy Spirit.

If you perceive something, take notice of it.

The Work of the Holy Spirit

John 16:13-15	When the Spirit of Truth comes, He will guide you into all truth. He will not be presenting his own ideas; he will be telling you what he has heard. He will tell you about the future. He will bring me glory by revealing to you whatever he receives from me. All that the Father has is mine; this is what I mean when I say that the Spirit will reveal to you whatever he receives from me.
John 16:24	Ask using my name, and you will receive; and you will have abundant joy.

Disclaimer

Statements regarding *Qigong for Christians* have not been evaluated by the FDA and are not intended to diagnose, treat, cure, or prevent any disease or health condition. The information in *Qigong for Christians* is intended to be educational and helpful in promoting one's spirituality. However, it is not intended as medical care or medical advice. Nor is it intended to replace the advice, services, or treatment of a medical doctor or medical professional. Before beginning any self-care regimen, it is advisable to consult with one's physician, especially pertaining to healthcare needs that require a medical diagnosis. The author and publisher are not responsible for any adverse effects rresulting from the application of information in Qigong for Christians. (2.), (3.)

The views and opinions of the author expressed in this material do not necessarily state or reflect those of Master Chunyi Lin and/or Spring Forest Qigong, and they may not be used for advertising or product endorsement purposes. Qigong is a secular activity in which the mind, body, and spirit are engaged to balance the body's energy and to promote healing. Master Chunyi Lin and/or Spring Forest Qigong do not promote or endorse any specific religion or religious belief.

Terminology Used in Qigong for Christians and Definitions

Qigong (Pronounced "chee gong") –
1.) An ancient Chinese exercise and healing technique that involves meditation, controlled breathing, and movement exercises.
2.) **Qigong** can be translated as "energy work" or "working with the life energy." (2.), (4.), (8.), (10.).

Qi (pronounced "chee") – A concept from traditional Chinese culture that means vital energy, information, breath, spirit, or life energy. (7.), (10.).

Dan tien – Energy center or important focal point in Qigong meditation.
The Lower Dan tien is located deep behind the navel. (2.), (5.), (6.), (9.).
The Middle Dan tien is located in the middle of the chest, in line with the lower area of the physical heart. In Qigong practice, when the term "heart" is used, it refers to the Middle Dan tien. (9.).

Procedure with Applicable Bible Verses

STEP 1

Sit comfortably. Have a bottle of water with you. Put a smile on your face.

Focus on your Lower Dan tien (the area deep behind your navel).

Visualize there is a beautiful light shining in your Lower Dan tien (you may visualize the light as a lit candle or another form of light).

Take three gentle, deep breaths.

While you are taking your deep breaths, scan your body from head to toe. As you do so, you are aware that every part of your body is right there with you. (2.) (4.), (5.), (6.).

Step 1 rationale:

In Qigong, the Lower Dan tien is a main energy center, containing life-giving vitality. In Qigong practice, light is healing. In scanning the body, we can become aware of energy blocks in our body.

As Christians, we acknowledge life and our inner light as a gift from God.

> John 1:1-5   In the beginning the Word already existed. He was with God, and He was God. He was in the beginning with God. He created everything there is. Nothing exists that He did not make. Life itself was in Him, and this Life gives Light to everyone. The Light shines through darkness, and the darkness can never extinguish it.

STEP 2

Notice your mind, heart, and spirit are right there, well-connected with your physical body. Take a moment to feel this.

Now, slowly bring your focus from your Lower Dan tien up to your heart. (As stated in the Terminology section on page 11, in Qigong practice, the term "Heart" refers to the Middle Dan tien located in the middle of the chest, in line with the lower area of your physical heart.) (9.).

Now, you visualize the light in your heart shining so beautifully.

This is the light of your unconditional love; this is the light of your soul. (2.), (4.), (5.), (6.).

Step 2 Rationale:

Qigong is a holistic approach which recognizes you as a whole person—heart, mind, body, and soul. The heart is an important energy center, which affects our overall health, and a powerful body organ, able to help with healing. (2.), (4.).

As Christians, we are called "Children of the Light" in the Bible, and we have God's divine power to live by God's principles; we are not of this world. (John 17:14-18 NLT; Colossians Theme, p 1465, NLT.).

John 12:36	Believe in the Light while there is still time; then you will become children of the Light.
John 12:46	I have come as a Light to shine in this dark world, so that all who trust in me will no longer remain in the darkness.

Mark 4:22-23	Everything that is now hidden or secret will eventually be brought to light. Anyone who is willing to hear should listen and understand...To those who are open to my teaching, more understanding will be given.
Romans 8:14	For all who are led by the Spirit of God are children of God.
1Corinthians 4:20	For the Kingdom of God is...living by God's power.

STEP 3

When you see this light, when you focus on this light, you feel such joy within you.

Now, as you focus on the light in your heart, tell the Lord what you pray for help with, in this meditation (i.e., it could be a physical or emotional or spiritual condition).

Also, tell the Lord what your life purpose is. If you do not know, ask the Lord to help you identify your life purpose. (4.), (5.), (6).

Step 3 Rationale:

In Qigong, we recognize that positive emotions such as joy, contentment, and gratitude give the heart more power to do its work in nurturing and healing the body (7.).

As Christians, we believe that joy is a gift of the Holy Spirit, and Jesus heals.

> John 8:12   I am the light of the world. If you follow me, you will not be stumbling through the darkness, because you will have the Light that leads to Life.
>
> John 3:21   Those who do what is right come to the Light gladly, so everyone can see that they are doing what God wants.
>
> Romans 14:17   For the Kingdom of God is…a matter of…living a life of goodness and peace and joy in the Holy Spirit.

STEP 4

Now, you call upon your healing Master Jesus Christ and pray to Him to support you in this meditation. When you are ready, you may say this prayer out loud.

Prayer:

Dear Lord Father God, Dear Lord Jesus, my healing Master,

Thank you for Your kindness, for Your love, for Your forgiveness, for Your guidance, and for Your healings and blessings in my life. At this moment with my heart so open, please send me even more of Your unconditional love to help me to open my heart more to You. Lord, please help me to open all my energy centers, all the energy channels, and all the energy blockages in my body, so I can be healed and balanced more completely. As I am healed, I will share my happiness, hope, love, joy, and peace more completely with my family, my friends, my community, and even with the world, and I thank you Lord. (4.), (5.), (6.).

Step 4 Rationale:

In Qigong, it is believed that love is the most powerful force in the universe and the most powerful frequency or vibration for healing ourselves and others. (2. p. 125) .

As Christians, we believe God is love.

> Romans 15:13   So I pray that God, who gives you Hope will keep you happy and full of Peace as you believe in Him. May you overflow with Hope through the power of the Holy Spirit.

Procedure with Applicable Bible Verses

Colossians 1:10-12 ...Do good kind things for others... You will learn to know God better and better. We pray...You will be strengthened with His glorious power...May you be filled with Joy, always thanking the Father, who has enabled you to share the inheritance that belongs to God's Holy people who live in the Light.

Colossians 3:12-15 ...Clothe yourselves with tenderhearted mercy, kindness, humility, gentleness, and patience. You must make allowance for each other's faults and forgive the person who offends you. Remember, the Lord forgave you, so you must forgive others. And the most important piece of clothing you must wear is Love. Love is what binds us all together in perfect harmony. And let the peace that comes from Christ rule in your hearts...You are all called to live in Peace. And always be thankful.

STEP 5

Now, you visualize the unconditional love of Master Jesus as a brilliant sun in the center of the sky above you.

Visualize the **Son** sending you beams of light into your heart, making the light in your heart even brighter. You feel your heart is so open, welcoming in this light. You feel your heart is being filled with God's perfect joy, pure love, and powerful healing energy. You feel how good you feel; how wonderful you feel. Now, take a moment to feel that. (4.), (5.), (6.).

Step 5 Rationale:

In Qigong, it is very important that we *feel* the healing process, rather than focusing on illness and negativity (6).

As Christians, we depend upon the power of the Holy Spirit that resides within us.

John 1:9	The one who is the true light, who gives light to everyone, was going to come into the world.
Matthew 4:16	The people who sat in darkness have seen a great light. And for those who lived in the land where death casts its shadow, a light has shined.
Colossians 1:27-29	For this is the secret: Christ lives in you, and this is your assurance that you will share in His glory...I depend on Christ's mighty power that works within me.
John 1:12-13	He is the one who baptizes with the Holy Spirit.

Procedure with Applicable Bible Verses

STEP 6

You feel your heart is full of God's perfect, healing light and healing energy.

Now, you send a beam of light from your heart into your bottle of water in front of you.

When you see the light get into the water, pray for the Lord to bless the water to help you to heal _____ (whatever your specific prayer for healing is).

Now, you may slowly drink the water, as you feel Jesus sending you His perfect unconditional love. As you feel the healing water flowing down your throat and into your body, you feel so grateful to the Lord Jesus Christ.

Now, you can put down the water. You may drink more either during or after this meditation. (4.), (5.), (6.).

Step 6 Rationale:

Visualization and the power of the mind are forms of energy that help with healing. (2. p.74).
Jesus heals and gives eternal life.

Acts 5:42	The Messiah you are looking for is Jesus.
John 6:20	I am here! Do not be afraid.
Acts 9:34	Aeneas, Jesus Christ heals you.
Acts 3:16	The name of Jesus has healed this man…Faith in Jesus' name has caused this healing…

Matthew 12:28	The Kingdom of God has arrived among you.
John 4:10, 14	Jesus said, I would give you living water...It becomes a perpetual Spring within them, giving them eternal Life.
John 6:35	Those who believe in me will never thirst.

Procedure with Applicable Bible Verses

STEP 7

At this time, bring your focus back onto your heart. Breathe gently and deeply. When you inhale, visualize you are breathing in God's divine healing love and energy as light coming in through every part of your body and collecting in your heart.

Then when you exhale, you visualize all the energy you do not need in your body changing into smoke and shooting out of every part of your body to the ends of the universe.

Feel God loving you and blessing you. Visualize God's divine, unconditional love and healing coming in through every pore of your body, collecting in your heart as light.

When you exhale, visualize all the energy you do not need in your body (such as worries, upsets, illness, pain, etc.) changing into smoke and shooting out of your body to the ends of the universe.

Take a few moments to continue inhaling God's healing light and exhaling the energy you no longer need. Breathe slowly and gently. (4.), (5.), (6.).

Step 7 Rationale:

In Qigong healing, the Qi, or energy, is transformed. The illness, which is also a form of energy, can be "transformed into something beautiful and blessing. (2. p.68).

God's healing power and miraculous wonders are ours through Jesus' holy name.

Acts 4:29-30	Give your servants great boldness in their preaching. Send your healing power; many miraculous signs and wonders be done through the name of your Holy servant Jesus.
2 Peter 2:3,4	As we know Jesus better, His divine power gives us everything we need for living a godly life. And by that same mighty power... He has promised that you...will share in his divine nature.
Luke 1:77-79	You will tell people how to find Salvation through forgiveness of their sins. Because of God's tender mercy the Light from heaven is about to break upon us to give Light to those who sit in darkness and in the shadow of death, And to guide us to the path of peace.

Procedure with Applicable Bible Verses

STEP 8

Choose to focus on one area where you feel you need healing.

Inhale, breathing in God's healing energy and love and light, coming into every part of your body and collecting into the area where you need healing.

Then exhale, breathing out the energy you do not need and transform it into smoke that shoots out of every part of your body to the ends of the universe.

Focus on the feeling of breathing in God's healing energy. Feel God blessing that part of your body where you need healing.

Exhale all the extra energy that you do not need; transform it into smoke and send it back into the universe.

How does it **feel** when God's light comes into your body where you need healing? **Feel** how good you feel, how wonderful you feel. (4.), (5.), (6.).

Step 8 Rationale:

Visualize and focus upon breathing in the healing energy from the universe and breathing out the illness, pain, sadness, etc., transforming it into smoke. (2. p.70-71).

We are transformed by the Holy Spirit leading us to the knowledge and glory of God.

Luke 2:30-32	I have seen the Savior you have given to all people. He is a light to reveal God to the Nations.

Luke 8:16-18	No one would light a lamp and then cover it up...to those who are open to my teaching, more understanding will be given...
Luke 10:9	The Kingdom of God is near you now.
Acts 3:12,13	And why look at us as though we had made this man walk by our own power and godliness? For it is the God...of all our ancestors who has brought glory to His servant Jesus by doing this.
Matthew 17:2-5	*The Transfiguration* Jesus' appearance changed so that his face shone like the Sun...
2 Corinthians 3:18	...We can be mirrors that brightly reflect the glory of the Lord. And as the Spirit of the Lord works within us, we become more and more like Him and reflect his glory even more.

STEP 9

Continue to breathe in God's healing love, energy, and light through every part of your body.

When you exhale, expel the excess energy, changing it into smoke and shooting it out to the ends of the universe. You feel so grateful to Christ Jesus, our healing Lord.

Breathe slowly and deeply. Breathe in God's healing light; transform the energy blockages into smoke.

Exhale and expel the excess energy, shooting it out of your body to the ends of the universe. (4.), (5.), (6.).

Step 9 Rationale:

Living a life based on love, kindness, and forgiveness is of utmost importance in order to achieve complete and perfect healing. (2. p.125).

Through choosing to forgive, we do not condone harmful acts; but through forgiveness, we let go of all bitterness, choosing the peace of Christ Jesus.

> Ephesians 4:31-32 — Get rid of all bitterness, rage, anger, harsh words, and slander, as well as all types of malicious behavior. Instead, be kind to each other, tender-hearted, forgiving one another, just as God through Christ has forgiven you.

John 1:12-13	But to all who believed Him and accepted Him, He gave the right to become children of God. They are reborn! This rebirth comes from God.
John 4:23-24	True worshipers will worship the Father in spirit and in truth...For God is spirit, so those who worship Him must worship in spirit, and in truth.

STEP 10

Now, focus back onto your heart; notice the light is shining in your heart. With each breath, the light gets bigger, brighter…bigger, brighter. The light continues to get bigger and brighter, and now, your whole body is enveloped in God's healing light.

Continue to breathe gently and deeply. Feel God's unconditional love flowing into every cell of your body. You see yourself in God's light…you are in God's light; God's light is in you. You and God's light are combined. (4.), (5.), (6.).

Step 10 Rationale:

A tool to wake up the inner-wisdom of your body:
Trust the universe; forget yourself.
The Qigong Password: "I am in the universe. The universe is in my body. The universe and I are combined together. (2 p. 105).
"God is Love, and all who live in Love live in God, and God lives in them" (1 John 4:16 NLT).

1 John 4:7	Dear Friends, let us continue to love one another, for love comes from God.
1 John 5:20	And now we are in God because we are in His Son, Jesus Christ. He is the only true God, and He is Eternal Life.
John 10:38	The Father is in me, and I am in the Father.
John 10:30	The Father and I are One.
Romans 5:5	For we know how dearly God loves us, because He has given us the Holy Spirit to fill our hearts with His Love.

STEP 11

Now, in God's light, open your healing energy channels, starting from your head. In the light, all energy channels open in your head. Now, your whole spine; all channels open, open, open. Upper spine, middle spine, lower spine, and tailbone. In the light, all channels open, open, open.

Upper chest, breasts, lungs, heart; all channels open in the light, open, open.

Stomach, liver, gall bladder, intestines, spleen, pancreas; all channels open, open, open.

Kidneys; all channels open, open, completely open.

Reproductive organs, all channels open, open, open.

Now, as the energy flows open up in your body; the energy channels open in the bottom of your torso and in your hips, your thighs and your knees; all channels open, open, completely open.

Now, down your legs, your calves, ankles, feet, and toes. In the light, all channels open, open, completely open.

And all channels open in your shoulders, your upper arms, your elbows. Open, open, completely open. Now, down your forearms, your wrists, your hands, and fingers; all channels open, open, completely open.

Now, with all your channels open in your body, You feel your body become lighter, lighter, and lighter still. (4.), (5.), (6.).

Step 11 Rationale:

"If we want to feel our best, we have to keep the energy channels open and the energy flowing smoothly and freely...All Sickness in your body, mind, or spirit are caused by energy blockages. Remove the blockage, and energy balance is restored. (2. p.85).

"I will give you back your health and heal your wounds, says the LORD." (Jeremiah 30: 17 NLT)

Isaiah 41:10	Don't be afraid, for I am with you. Do not be dismayed, for I am your God. I will strengthen you. I will help you. I will uphold you with my victorious right hand.
3 John 1:2	Dear friend, I am praying that all is well with you and that your body is as healthy as I know your soul is.
Philippians 4:19	And my God will meet all your needs according to the riches of his glory in Christ Jesus.
Psalms 30:2	O LORD my God, I cried out to you for help, and you restored my health.
Psalms 103:2-3	Praise the LORD, I tell myself, and never forget the good things He does for me. He forgives all my sins and heals all my diseases.
Matthew 13:12	To those who are open to my teaching, more understanding will be given, and they will have an abundance of knowledge...

Matthew 13:17   Many prophets and godly people have longed to see and hear what you have seen and heard, but they could not.

STEP 12

Now, let us give thanks to our Master Healer, Jesus Christ; and we will end our meditation in prayer.

Dear Lord Father God, Dear Lord Jesus,

We praise and thank you for being our healing Master and for participating with us in our healing meditation. Thanks be to God for allowing us, Your children, to partake in Your divine nature and for so graciously bestowing upon us the gifts of the Holy Spirit. Glory be to God through Jesus Christ—our Healer, our Savior, our Redeemer, the Messiah, King of Kings, the Ancient of Days, now and forever.

In Jesus' holy precious name,

God the Father, the Son, and the Holy Spirit, amen and amen!

Step 12 Rationale:

Qigong: Live in gratitude. "Don't focus on material things at the expense of spiritual things. Keep all things in their proper balance." (2. p.95)

Bible: "Always be joyful. Keep on praying...Always be thankful, for this is God's will for you who belong to Christ Jesus" (1 Thessalonians 5:16-18, NLT).

Luke 24:47	With my authority, take this message of repentance to all The nations... There is forgiveness of sins for all who turn to me.

Luke 24:49	I will send the Holy Spirit to fill you with power from Heaven.
Matthew 13:43	The godly will shine like the Sun in their Father's Kingdom.
Luke 11:33-34, 36	No one lights a lamp and then hides it or puts it under a basket. Instead it is put on a lampstand to give light to all who enter the room. Your eyes are a lamp for your body. A pure eye lets sunshine into your soul…If you are filled with light, with no dark corners, then your whole life will be radiant, as though a floodlight is shining on you.
Luke 12:29-31	Your Father already knows your needs. He will give you all you need from day to day if you make the Kingdom of God your primary concern…it gives your Father great happiness to give you the Kingdom.
Luke 17:21	For the Kingdom of God is among you.
Colossians 3:1	…You have been raised to New Life with Christ…

Bibliography

1. *The Book Holy Bible New Living Translation.* Tyndale House Publishers, Inc., 1996, Carol Stream, Illinois 60188.
Scripture quotations are taken from the Holy Bible, New Living Translation, copyright c 1996, 2004, 2007, 2013 by Tyndale House Foundation. Used by permission of Tyndale House publishers, Inc., Carol Stream, Illinois 60188. All rights reserved.
2. Chunyi Lin. *Born a Healer*, Spring Forest Publishing, United States, October, 2005.
3. MasterChunyiLin.www.bornahealer.com
4. MasterChunyiLin.www.springforestqigong.com.
5. Master Chunyi Lin. Healing Connection audio tele-seminar, "Loving Without Conditions." www.springforestqigong.com. August, 2018.
6. Master Chunyi Lin. Healing Connection audio tele-seminar, "Moving through the Season—The Best Movements to Open Your Heart." www.springforestqigong.com. July 24, 2018.
7. Master Chunyi Lin, Healing Connection audio tele-seminar, "Heart of Joy." www.springforestqigong.com. February, 2019.
8. Master Chunyi Lin. Healing Connection audio tele-seminar, "Gratitude for the Soul." www.springforestqigong.com.

9. Master Chunyi Lin, Healing Connection, audio tele-seminar, "What is the 'Spirits of all Beings?'" www.springforestqigong.com. July, 2019.
10. What is Qigong? LiveScience38192-qigong.html cited 9-24-18.
11. Wikipedia. en.m.wikipedia.org, online, cited 9-24-18
12. Wikipedia. wikipedia.org/wiki/Qigong, online, cited 3-29-19
13. Wikipedia, "The Free Encyclopedia" (English), The Wikimedia Foundation, Inc. online, cited 6-15-19